I Know There's a Power

First published October 1991.

Copyright © 1991, P. K. Hallinan
All rights reserved. No portion of this publication
may be reproduced in any manner without the written
permission of the publisher.

ISBN: 0-89486-780-6

Printed in the United States of America.

Library of Congress Catalog Card Number: 91-73228

ABOUT P. K. HALLINAN

Patrick Hallinan began writing children's books at the request of his wife, who asked him to create an original Christmas gift for their two young sons. Today, nearly twenty years later, P. K. Hallinan is one of America's foremost authors of children's books that teach personal values and self-esteem to young readers. His sensitive text and heart-warming illustrations offer a celebration of life to all who visit his very special world.

Although Mr. Hallinan writes primarily for children, his books manage to touch the child in all of us. It's this ability that enables Hallinan's books to be enjoyed by all children, young and old, who see the world through the eyes of innocence.

Mr. Hallinan lives with his wife, Jeanne, and their three dogs in Ashland, Oregon. He is the author of thirty children's books, including *Easy Does It, One Day at a Time, Live and Let Live, I Know Who I Am,* and *I Know I Belong*—all published by Hazelden Educational Materials.

I Know There's a Power

P.K. Hallinan

HAZELDEN

I know there's a Power
greater than I
that carves out the mountains . . .

and paints in the sky . . .

whose love brings the sunlight
in soft morning hours
with songbirds that sing out,
"I know there's a Power."

There are times made for laughter . . .

and times made for tears.

There are days I'll know bravery . . .

and days I'll know fear.

But life has a balance that always maintains although we have losses, we also have gains.

I know there is wisdom far greater than mine—wisdom to guide me through difficult times.

So when I feel lost
or adrift at loose ends . . .

I'll turn to a teacher,
a parent . . .

or friends.

And if they can't help me,
I'll try to set free
all of the problems
that are too big for me.

We all have our setbacks.

We all have our glory.

We all make mistakes
as we play out our story.

But this much is certain:
Whatever the task,
doing our best
is the best we can ask.

I'm glad there are rainbows to follow a storm.

I'm glad that in springtime the world is reborn.

I'm especially glad
that even at night
our path is made clear
when we follow the light.

But as sure as a rainfall brings life to the flowers, I know that I'm loved, and . . .

I know there's a Power.